Why is the Arctic so cold? What did the first people of the Arctic eat? How do polar bears cross thin ice? What other animals make the Arctic their home?

Find out the answers to these questions and more in . . .

Magic Tree House®
Research Guide
POLAR BEARS
AND THE ARCTIC

A nonfiction companion to
Polar Bears Past Bedtime

It's Jack and Annie's very own guide to the Arctic.

Including:
• Animal adaptations
• Arctic people
• Hibernation
• Polar bear safety
And much more!

Here's what people are saying about the Magic Tree House® Research Guides:

Your Research Guides are a great addition to the Magic Tree House series! I have used Rain Forests *and* Space *as "read-alouds" during science units. Thank you for these!!*—Cheryl M., teacher

My eight-year-old son thinks your books are great—and I agree. I wish my high school students had read the Research Guides when they were his age. —John F., parent and teacher

And from the Magic Tree House® Web site:

My son loves the Research Guides about knights, pirates, and mummies. He has even asked for a notebook, which he takes with him to the museum for his research.—A parent

The Research Guides have been very helpful to us, as our daughter has an abundance of questions. Please come out with more. They help us help her find the answers to her questions!—An appreciative mom and dad

I love your books. I have a great library at home filled with your books and Research Guides. The [Knights and Castles] *Research Guide really helped me do a report on castles and knights!*—A young reader

Magic Tree House® Research Guide

POLAR BEARS
AND THE ARCTIC

A nonfiction companion to
Polar Bears Past Bedtime

by Mary Pope Osborne
and Natalie Pope Boyce

illustrated by Sal Murdocca

A STEPPING STONE BOOK™
Random House 🏠 New York

www.magictreehouse.com
www.randomhouse.com/kids

Educators and librarians, for a variety of teaching tools, visit us at
www.randomhouse.com/teachers

Library of Congress Cataloging-in-Publication Data
Osborne, Mary Pope.
Polar bears and the Arctic : a nonfiction companion to polar bears past
bedtime / by Mary Pope Osborne and Natalie Pope Boyce ;
illustrated by Sal Murdocca. — 1st ed.
    p.   cm. — (Magic tree house research guide) "A stepping stone book."
Includes bibliographical references and index.
ISBN 978-0-375-83222-2 (trade) — ISBN 978-0-375-93222-9 (lib. bdg.)
1. Polar bear—Arctic regions—Juvenile literature. 2. Arctic regions—Juvenile
literature. I. Boyce, Natalie Pope. II. Murdocca, Sal, ill. III. Title.
QL737.C27083 2007 599.786—dc22 2006022306

Printed in the United States of America
10 9 8 7 6 5
First Edition

For Sally Hatch

Scientific Consultant:

JAMES J. BREHENY, Vice President and Director, Bronx Zoo.

Anthropological Consultant:

STEVE HENRIKSON and MARTHA CROW, Alaska State Museum.

Education Consultant:

HEIDI JOHNSON, Earth Science and Paleontology, Lowell Junior High School, Bisbee, Arizona.

Very special thanks to Paul Coughlin for his photographs; to our wonderful illustrator, Sal Murdocca; and to everyone on the team at Random House: Joanne Yates Russell, Gloria Cheng, Mallory Loehr, and our great editor, Diane Landolf, whose excellent good sense always keeps us on track.

POLAR BEARS
AND THE ARCTIC

Contents

Dear Readers,

Our adventures with <u>Polar Bears Past Bedtime</u> made us wonder what it is like to live in the Arctic. How is it possible for humans and animals to survive in such a freezing-cold place? We gathered up our notebooks and pencils and set off for the library. It was time to research!

The librarians helped us choose the very best books. It was snowing when we got home. We fixed a cup of tea and began to read. Then we went to our computers and found great articles on Arctic animals and life in the Arctic. We

learned that Arctic animals have extra fat and fur to trap in heat. We found out how early people in the Arctic sometimes lived in houses made of ice. We printed out our information and sat down to take notes. The notes grew into a book. And now, dear reader, it's your turn to learn what we learned about polar bears and the Arctic. Hope you enjoy it!

Jack
Annie

1

Polar Bears
and the Arctic

It is night at the North Pole. A giant bear plods across the ice. At times he stops to sniff the air. Overhead green and blue lights flicker in the dark sky. The world is silent. It is the beginning of winter. Soon the sun will not shine for months.

As the bear walks, he swings his head from side to side. His paws, as big as dinner plates, make no sound on the hard, cold ice.

The Arctic Ocean is the smallest ocean in the world.

The bear lies down for a nap. He can hear ice in the Arctic Ocean creaking and groaning. The bear turns over and covers his nose with his paw to keep it warm.

The polar bear's world is strange and beautiful. He lives in the Arctic, near the North Pole, the most northern tip of the world. The Arctic Ocean covers the North Pole.

Most of the Arctic Ocean is frozen into a huge mass of ice called the *polar ice cap.* The polar ice cap reaches about 500 miles down from the North Pole.

All of what we call the Arctic lies within the *Arctic Circle,* which is an imaginary circle around the North Pole. It includes the Arctic Ocean. But it also includes the northern parts of Alaska,

Canada, Russia, Norway, Sweden, Finland, and Iceland, as well as most of Greenland.

The Arctic does not all look the same. Parts are flat and bare. But other places have tall mountains, lakes, and rivers. There are even villages, towns, and cities within the Arctic Circle.

People have lived in the Arctic for thousands of years. They have learned how to exist in this harsh setting.

Arctic animals can also live in this icy world where water freezes in seconds and few plants grow. These animals survive where the land is frozen all year long.

Barrow, Alaska

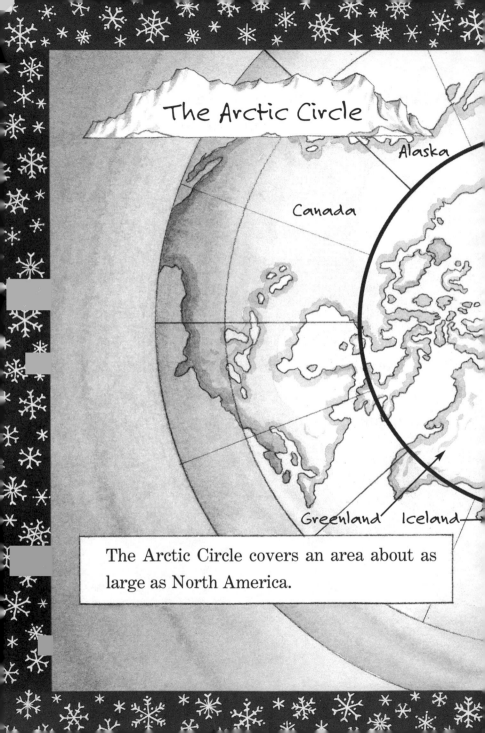

The Arctic Circle

Alaska

Canada

Greenland   Iceland

The Arctic Circle covers an area about as large as North America.

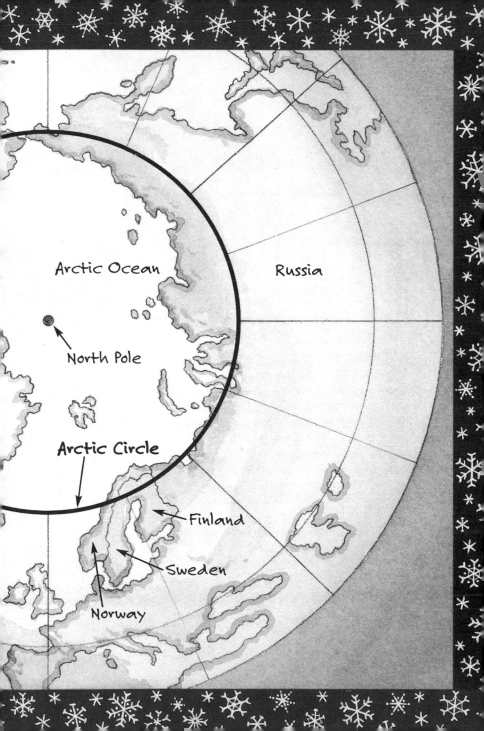

2

The Arctic

The area closest to the North Pole is called the *High Arctic*. It is the coldest part of the Arctic Circle. The land is flat and dry. The soil is too poor for plants or trees to grow. Few land animals can live in the High Arctic.

The other part of the Arctic is called the *Low Arctic*. The Low Arctic is farther from the North Pole. Plants cover about 90 percent of the land there. Many animals live in the Low Arctic.

A large part of the Arctic is called *tundra*. Tundra is flat, dry land without trees.

Tundra makes up about 20 percent of the land in the world.

Tundra comes from a Finnish word meaning "treeless plain."

The Arctic tundra covers the southern coasts of Greenland and the northern parts of Alaska, Canada, Europe, and Russia. A lot of the soil in the tundra stays frozen all year. It is called *permafrost* (PER-muh-frawst). Since the land is frozen, water cannot drain. It remains frozen in ponds and bogs.

Why Is the Arctic So Cold?

Brrrr! The Arctic is super-cold most of the time. We say the weather is *freezing* when it is thirty-two degrees Fahrenheit or below. That's when water turns into ice. In January and February, the Arctic is about twenty-nine degrees *below* zero!

When it's this cold, your spit freezes before it hits the ground. You spit ice balls!

It is very cold in the Arctic for several reasons. One is that the sun does not shine directly over the Arctic. It shines right above the *equator* (ih-KWAY-tur). The equator is an imaginary line that runs around the middle of the earth. Countries near the equator are warm and sunny.

Because the sun's rays have to travel so far to reach the Arctic, they lose heat.

Snow and ice cause even more cooling. Light colors reflect the sun's rays back into space. And because ice and snow are so cold, they cool the air above the land.

The Arctic is also very dry. Cold air traps less moisture than warm air. Scientists call the Arctic "the polar desert"!

Why the Arctic Is Freezing

Sun's rays travel far

Ice and snow reflect heat

Ice and snow chill air

Land of the Midnight Sun

The Arctic is known as the *Land of the Midnight Sun*. For two months in the summer, the sun doesn't set. It shines twenty-four hours a day.

The reason for this is the tilt, or angle, of the planet Earth in relation to the sun. As Earth travels around the sun, it very slowly begins to tip toward the sun in the summer. Then it tilts away from the sun in the winter.

During an Arctic summer, the North Pole faces the sun. The sun shines all through the day and night.

The path Earth travels around the sun is called its <u>orbit</u>.

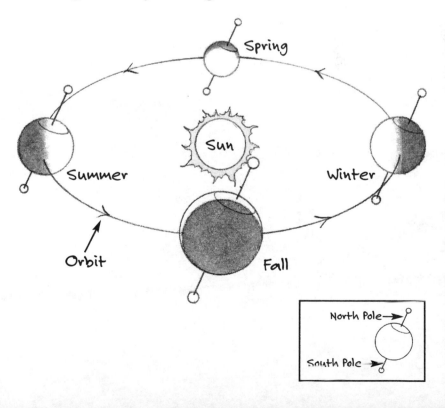

Northern Lights

The fall and spring skies in the North often light up with beautiful blue, green, red, and violet lights. The lights seem to play with the darkness. They pulse, crackle, and streak. We call these lights the *northern lights*, or *aurora borealis* (uh-ROAR-uh BORE-ee-AA-lus).

Aurora was the Roman goddess of dawn. *Borealis* comes from Boreas, the Greek god of the north wind.

The northern lights happen when energy particles (PAR-tih-kulz) from the sun hit the air far above the earth. These particles collide with gases that surround the earth. Energy is given off and appears in the sky as colorful lights.

Particles are tiny pieces of a larger object.

South Pole

The coldest weather of all is at the South Pole. The *continent* of *Antarctica* (ant-ARK-tih-kuh) covers the South Pole. A continent is a big landmass. North America and Australia are examples of other continents.

Antarctica is almost completely covered by a layer of ice one mile thick. It is so cold and dry that except for scientists, no one actually lives there. The scientists live in specially built research stations. The lowest temperature ever recorded in the world was in Antarctica . . . 128.6 degrees below zero!

Antarctica is home to animals like penguins, seals, whales, and fish. Polar bears don't live in Antarctica, and penguins don't live in the Arctic. They have to go to zoos to meet one another!

3

First People
of the Arctic

The first people came to the Arctic
thousands of years ago. They settled in
groups in northern Alaska, Scandinavia,
Canada, and Siberia, and along the coast of
Greenland. These groups spoke languages
that are a lot alike. They also shared many
of the same customs.

These people are often called *Eskimos*.
This is not a name that they chose for

themselves. So today many Arctic people want to be known by the name of their group, like the *Inuit* (IH-noo-wut) of Canada and Greenland or the *Yup'ik* (YOO-pik) of Alaska.

Frigid means "extremely cold."

For thousands of years, native Arctic people battled *frigid* temperatures, bitterly cold winds, and rough seas. But even though life was hard, they learned the secrets of survival in a frozen world.

Hunting and Fishing

Much of their food came from the Arctic Ocean. They hunted whales, seals, and walruses and fished for salmon, cod, and other sea creatures.

A caribou is a kind of reindeer.

On land they also followed the great herds of *caribou* (KARE-uh-boo) that roamed the Arctic. They ate caribou

meat and used the skins for tents and
clothing.

This Arctic native is dragging a seal
home from the hunt.

Hunt Like an Arctic Native

If you want to hunt and fish like the native people of Alaska did, this is what you do:

    1. Fish in a small boat made of leather. Carry several harpoons with you.

Clothing

Arctic people wore clothes made of animal skins. Women made clothes from caribou or

2. Wait for many hours at a hole in the ice for a seal or walrus to come up for air.

3. In the summer, follow herds of caribou for many miles with bows and arrows.

seal. They sewed with needles carved from animal bones and thread made from animal *tendons.* Tendons are a kind of stringy tissue that connects muscles to bone or other muscles.

Everyone wore mittens, boots, pants, and heavy jackets with hoods called *parkas*. Mothers made their parka hoods large enough to fit over the babies they carried on their backs.

This is an Arctic native in a parka.

Dogsleds

Arctic people knew that at different times of the year, some places were better than others for hunting or fishing. They traveled to these places even though they did not have cars or roads.

On land, everyone traveled in dogsleds made from driftwood or animal bones. Two to twelve dogs pulled the sleds. The dogs' owners and their families rode in the sleds or ran along beside them.

Sometimes parts of the sled were even made from dried salmon.

37

Sled dogs are very hardy and can live outside in the coldest weather. Good sled dogs pull two times their weight. They can travel for many miles without getting tired.

Sled dogs also helped their owners find food. They would spot seals as they came up to breathe in the ice holes. And when other animals came too close, the sled dogs would fight to defend their owners.

I wonder why sled dogs have tails that curl up.

Let me guess! That's so their tails don't freeze and stick out straight behind them!

Kayak

Kayaks and Umiaks

On the sea, people used two kinds of boats.
One boat was the *kayak* (KY-ack). They are
small one-man boats used for hunting small
sea animals and fish. We still use kayaks
today, though mostly for fun.

Kayaks move quietly in the water.
Wearing special waterproof clothes made
from walrus intestine, hunters sneaked up
on their prey.

A larger boat made of animal skins and bones was called an *umiak* (OO-mee-ack). It could hold about twenty people. The umiak carried men out to hunt the great whales.

Umiaks

Houses

Arctic people had several types of houses. In the summer, many lived in tents made of animal skins.

During the winter, they moved into sod houses built into the earth. They covered the houses with animal skins to keep out the cold winds. The front door usually slanted down to the outside. This trapped the cold air and kept it from blowing into the house. This type of doorway is called an *arctic entrance.*

Sod is made up of dirt, grass, and roots.

When some groups traveled in the winter, they built ice houses we now call *igloos*. Using special ice knives, they chopped the ice and snow into blocks. Then they fitted the blocks together to form a round ice house. Igloos could be put up in one day . . . or even one hour!

Igloo comes from the Inuit word iglu, which means "house."

Inside their houses, families lit oil lamps. The oil was made from whale or walrus fat. At night when the winds howled outside, they huddled together. The adults told stories and carved beautiful objects from bone and ivory.

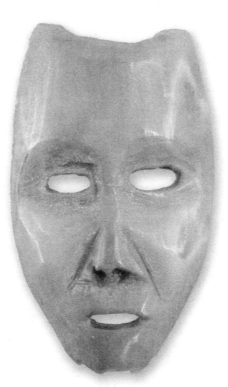

The Tyara maskette was carved over 2,600 years ago.

Families

Families lived in groups of about one hundred. The men hunted, fished, built houses, and made weapons and tools.

The women took charge of making clothes, cleaning, and taking care of the children. They also prepared food, and they dried fish and meat for storage.

Children were rarely punished. Although they had fun, they also had to work. They helped their parents hunt and gather food. They also collected driftwood to use for sleds and houses.

The Argument Contest

An <u>insult</u> is something said that is mean or bad about someone else.

When people got angry with one another, one way they solved arguments was to have an "insult contest."

They would stand up and yell insults

44

back and forth. The first to lose his or her temper lost the contest.

Arctic Stories

For native Arctic people, many things had souls or magic powers. They had sacred stories about the wind, animals, the aurora borealis, the sea, and more.

Because they saw polar bears walking upright, they told stories about polar bears that lived and talked like humans.

Some groups told stories about Sedna, a sea goddess. They believed Sedna lived on the bottom of the sea. All the sea creatures obeyed her. Fishermen tried to keep Sedna happy. If not, they worried fishing could be really bad!

Arctic natives also believed certain people had magic powers. They called them *shamans* (SHAH-munz). Shamans acted as doctors as well as advice givers.

This photo from around 1910 shows a shaman driving away evil spirits from a sick boy.

Native People Today

Over the years, life in the Arctic has changed. The Arctic is rich in oil, gas, fish, and minerals. Miners, fishermen, fur traders, and others have joined Arctic natives to make the Arctic their home.

Today, in spite of many changes, some native people follow the old ways of their ancestors. They live in small villages, get their food from the sea, and speak their own languages. They still honor many of their old customs. Some even travel by dogsled.

But many native people do twenty-first-century things as well. They drive snowmobiles, motorboats, and cars. And many live in modern houses and buy food in stores.

Native Arctic people have a great history. And they are proud to be related to the first people who dared to make the frozen Arctic their home.

This modern Inuit family lives on Ellesmere Island, Canada.

Susan Butcher and the Iditarod

When Susan Butcher was a little girl, she lived in the city. But she always dreamed about living in the country and owning lots of dogs. When Susan grew up, her dream came true. She took off for the wilds of Alaska. Susan began to train sled dogs. It wasn't long before she became a champion *musher*.

Mushers train and race sled dogs.

Each year there is a famous dogsled race from Anchorage to Nome, Alaska, called the *Iditarod* (eye-DID-uh-rod). It covers roughly 1,150 icy miles. Usually sixty-five or more mushers race with twelve to sixteen dogs to a sled.

Icy winds howl as the mushers and their dogs dash through the countryside, towns, and villages. Temperatures can drop to fifty degrees below zero. Sometimes it takes weeks to finish the race.

Susan Butcher won the Iditarod four times. But once she almost didn't finish. She and her dogs were attacked by a cranky moose!

This is Susan Butcher and her team.

4

Arctic Animals

Arctic animals need special protection against the freezing weather. Many have several layers of thick fur coats. The inner layer keeps them warm. The outer layer keeps them dry. Arctic animals also have extra layers of fat that trap in the heat.

Moving around on snow or ice is difficult. Some animals, like the polar bear, have big feet. Their feet act like snowshoes and keep them from crashing through the snow.

Hibernation

Some Arctic animals escape the icy winter by curling up in their dens. They drift into what seems like a deep sleep for most of the winter. But they are not actually sleeping; they are *hibernating* (HY-bur-nate-ing).

All summer long, animals like the female polar bear and the Arctic hare eat as much food as they can. When winter arrives, they dig dens out of snow or leaves. Sometimes they find shelter in a cave. Then they curl up and become very still.

Adult male polar bears do not hibernate.

The Arctic ground squirrel hibernates for six months.

Hibernating saves the animals a lot of energy. Their heartbeat slows down. Their body temperature lowers. They breathe very slowly. The Arctic ground squirrel's body temperature is the lowest

54

of all hibernating animals. It falls below freezing!

Sometimes hibernating animals leave their dens for a short time to find food. Then they head back to their warm dens and hibernate some more.

Migration

To escape the cold, many animals *migrate* in the fall. When animals migrate, they travel to distant places that are warmer. The animals return home in the spring when the temperature rises.

Some animals travel really great distances. But no animal migrates as far as the *Arctic tern*. It flies more than 21,750 miles back and forth from the Arctic to Antarctica. That's like flying between New York City and Los Angeles about eight times!

Arctic tern

A gray whale lunges up to the ocean surface in Baja, Mexico.

Some sea creatures migrate as well. Gray whales swim over 12,000 miles from the Arctic to the coast of sunny Mexico.

Changing Colors

To protect themselves from *predators*, some animals have fur that changes color during the year. In the summer, their fur is darker and blends into the grasses and shrubs. In the winter, their fur is as white as snow.

Arctic hare
in winter

Arctic hare
in summer

Animals like Arctic foxes, hares, and weasels are gray or brown in the summer. In the winter, they are completely white. This really confuses any predator that is looking for a tasty meal!

Let's mush on and meet our favorite Arctic animals!

Lemming

Lemmings are *really* important in the Arctic because so many animals depend on them for food.

Lemmings look like hamsters. They burrow together in tunnels under the snow. In the summer, their coats are brown. In the winter, they turn white, and their feet actually grow larger to help them get around.

60

When their food runs out or they get too crowded, lemmings hit the road to find a new place to live. People have been amazed to see thousands rushing through meadows and woods at breakneck speed.

Sometimes they race into dangerous streams or rivers. Hundreds drown in their haste to find new homes. They've even been known to fall off cliffs!

Arctic Hare

Arctic hares have long back legs and smaller ears than other hares. They are super-speedy. They stand up on their back legs and look around for predators. If they see one, they take off at speeds of more than thirty miles per hour.

It's not unusual to see about 200 Arctic hares gathered together. But they don't cuddle up. They stay three feet apart. If one wanders too close to another, it gets attacked!

Like lemmings, Arctic hares are the favorite food for many animals. Their biggest danger comes from snowy owls, Arctic foxes, and Arctic wolves.

Wolverine

Wolverines are not wolves; they are large weasels. They live in North America, Europe, and Asia, as well as in the Arctic tundra. Native Americans called wolverines "evil spirits" because they are very fierce. And some people call them "skunk bears" because they are so smelly.

Wolverines eat small animals, plants, and birds. But they also kill larger animals like deer and caribou.

Wolverines have very sharp teeth and strong jaws. They growl and show their teeth to keep wolves and other animals away from their kills. They are truly one of the fiercest animals in the Arctic . . . or just about anywhere!

Arctic Wolf

Arctic wolves are smaller than other wolves. Their coats remain white all year. They hunt in small packs for deer, caribou, or other animals. During a chase, they can run up to forty-five miles per hour.

The wolves surround their prey and bring it down with a quick bite on the neck. Then they gulp the meat in big chunks. Sometimes they eat up to twenty pounds of meat at a time!

Did anyone ever tell you not to "wolf down" your food?

Wolves howl a lot. They greet each other by howling. They howl to gather the pack for a hunt. They howl to warn each other of danger or to tell each other where they are. Some people have seen wolves howling for no reason at all. They just seemed to be singing together.

Narwhal

Narwhals are most unusual whales. The males have a very, very long left tooth. It grows out of their mouths in a spiral. And it grows to be seven to ten feet long!

Narwhals use their tusks for fighting or for finding food. In the summer, male narwhals rub their tusks together. This is called "tusking." Scientists aren't sure why they do this. Perhaps it's their way of communicating.

Many people believe the myth of the unicorn grew out of narwhal sightings. That's why today we often call narwhals "unicorn whales," or "unicorns of the sea."

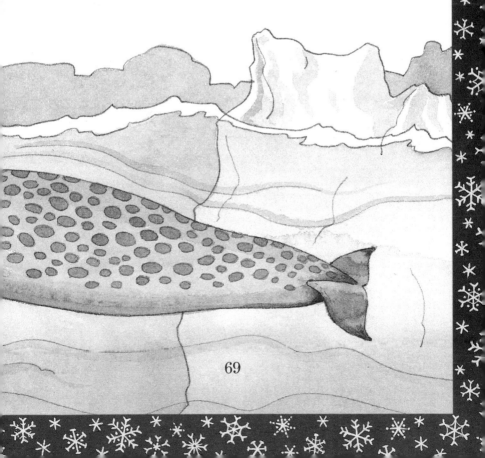

Snowy Owl

Snowy owls are different from other owls. Most owls are *nocturnal* (nock-TUR-nul) and hunt only at night. Snowy owls hunt mostly during the day. They use sharp claws called "talons" to capture their prey.

Snowy owls have tufts of feathers on either side of their big yellow eyes. These feathers force sound back into the owl's ears. When the owls fly high above the ground, they can see and hear a mouse far down below.

These big white owls swoop down upon their prey without making a sound. They grab it with their talons and gobble it down whole. When mothers arrive back at their nests, they cough up what they've eaten . . . right into their babies' mouths!

Seal

There are eighteen different types of seals. They can be found in every ocean and even in some lakes. Seals give birth on land. Otherwise, they spend all their lives in the water.

Seals are great divers. Although they are clumsy on land, they are sleek and fast in the water. Seals can stay underwater for thirty minutes! Their heartbeat slows down underwater. This allows them to use less oxygen and stay underwater for a longer time.

When seals need to breathe, they come to the surface. They either chew holes in the ice or hit it with their heads to make an air hole. Then they take big gulps of fresh air.

Seals eat fish, birds, shellfish, and tiny shrimp-like creatures called "krill."

Walrus

Walruses are huge seals. They live both on land and in the sea. Thick layers of blubber, or fat, lie underneath their skin to keep them warm. Males can weigh up to 3,000 pounds. That's as much as a small car!

Males use their tusks for fighting. Tusks are also handy for breaking up the ice. When male walruses rest in the water, they hook their tusks over an ice floe so they won't sink. Then they take a snooze.

Walruses find their food on the ocean floor. Their long whiskers help them feel around on the bottom. They eat clams, crabs, fish, sea cucumbers, and worms.

Walrus mothers and babies nap on ice floes. If a mother senses danger, she grabs her baby with her flippers, holds it tightly to her chest, and dives into the water.

5

Polar Bears

Polar bears are the largest land predators on earth. They can do amazing things. They can smell a seal from miles away. They can run at speeds of over twenty-six miles an hour for short distances. And they can swim for up to sixty miles without resting.

When they eat, they sometimes pack away one hundred pounds of meat at one sitting. And even though they are huge, they can walk across very thin ice without breaking through. If the ice is super-thin, they can spread their entire body out and inch across the surface. That is pretty amazing!

Really Big Bears

Polar bears have strong shoulders, big feet, and powerful front legs. Male bears often weigh over a thousand pounds. They can grow up to eleven feet long. When they stand up, they are as tall as a one-story building!

Female bears are not as large as males. They grow to about eight feet in length and sometimes reach seven hundred pounds.

The Perfect Winter Coat

Most people think polar bears are white. Actually their fur is not white. Each hair is a clear hollow tube. The hairs reflect light and make the bears look white.

The hollow tubes soak up warmth and direct heat into the bear's skin. The air trapped in the tubes also helps the bears float in water . . . just like inner tubes.

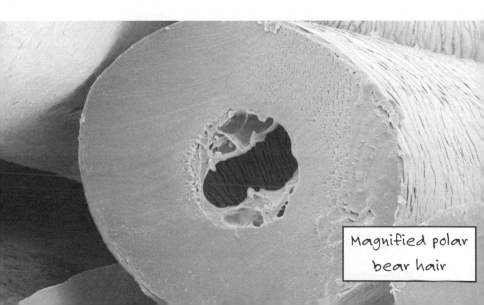

Magnified polar bear hair

The bears' outer hair is oily and slick. When they shake themselves, ice and water slide right off. Polar bears are waterproof!

Polar bears have a second layer of thick fur . . . like the warm clothes you wear under your winter coats. This fur also traps air and keeps the bears warm.

You might be surprised to know that polar bears have black skin. Black absorbs heat. But the bears don't seem black because their fur is thick and close together.

On sunny days, the bears' body temperature is about ninety-eight degrees . . . about the same as people's.

Fur and small bumps on the bottom of their feet help the bears grip the ice.

Four inches of blubber lie right underneath the skin. Blubber is also very good at holding in heat.

Polar bears keep so much heat in their bodies that when they run, they can actually overheat . . . even in the freezing Arctic. When they are filmed with an *infrared* (IN-fruh-red) camera, the picture shows no heat escaping at all. It's all stored in the bears' bodies.

An **infrared** **camera** photographs the heat that an object gives off.

In the summer, the bears gradually lose their old coats. New coats then begin to grow for next winter.

Polar Bears in Singapore Turn Green!

In 2004, zookeepers at the Singapore Zoo were shocked when a polar bear named Sheba and her son, Inuka, began to turn green! Singapore is a hot, humid country.

The keepers discovered *algae* (AL-jee) growing in the bears' hair shafts. Algae are very teeny green plants that grow in hot, damp places. After a good bath, Sheba and Inuka looked white again.

Sheba and Inuka

Swimming Champs

Scientists call polar bears *Ursus maritimus* (UR-sus mare-uh-TEEM-us). This means "sea bear" in Latin. Polar bears are at home in the sea as well as on land. Much of the time, they live and hunt on ice floes bobbing in the Arctic Ocean. They have to be super-strong swimmers. People have spotted polar bears swimming sixty miles from land.

Swimming bear

The polar bear's long neck helps hold its head above the water.

Their big paws help them in the water. The paws are about a foot wide. A little bit of webbing between the toes helps push the water aside as they swim. Polar bears paddle with their huge front paws while their back paws do the steering.

Polar bears can dive fifteen feet underwater and stay under for two minutes. Their nostrils close to keep the water out. When they get back on land, they shake the water off, just like dogs.

Okay, so how do polar bears cross thin ice without breaking through?

They use their big feet to spread their weight out evenly over the ice.

Their Noses Know

Polar bears have great noses! When they want to get a really good whiff of something, they stand up on their back legs and sniff the air.

They can smell a seal lying under several feet of ice from a mile away. They can smell dead animals up to twenty miles away!

They can smell you as well. And that might make them *very* hungry! Polar bears will attack people. They are extremely dangerous. They might be fun to watch, but they are not friendly! Polar bears kill more people for food than any other bears.

Warning: they hiss before they attack.

Diet

Polar bears are *carnivorous* (kar-NIHV-ur-us). This means that they eat meat.

Carnivorous comes from the Latin word for "meat," which is <u>carnis</u>.

85

Seals make up most of their diet. If they don't have any luck catching seals, they will

 A polar bear successfully grabs its prey.

eat ducks, small rodents, fish, and even people's garbage. The bears will also eat any dead walruses, caribou, and whales they come across.

Teeth

Polar bears have forty-two sharp teeth. They can easily bite into tough hides and cut through blubber and flesh. The bears usually don't chew their food. They swallow it in huge gulps. So don't eat like a wolf *or* a bear! Although meat is the main part of their diet, people have spotted polar bears nibbling on seaweed and berries as well.

Hunting

Polar bears grab seals as they come up to breathe through holes in the ice. Some bears will wait by holes for hours or even

A bear quietly waits for dinner to appear.

days! When the seal appears, the bear drags it, quick as lightning, to the surface.

On land, the bears creep up behind the seals *very* carefully. They walk so softly that they don't make a sound. When they get close enough, they charge in for the kill.

In the spring, ringed seals give birth in caves under the snow. The mother seal digs the cave near an ice hole.

If a bear hears or smells seal pups in the den, she'll smash the cave in with her powerful front paws and gobble up the pups.

When polar bears kill an animal, the first

things they eat are the skin and the fat. Sometimes the bears don't eat the entire kill. They eat their fill and then wander off.

After they eat, polar bears clean up. They wash themselves with snow or water. They don't just wash their faces; they roll around and get clean all over.

Polar Bear Safety

Many polar bears live in Canada. If you visit a park there, you might run across some bears. They are not friendly pets! These rules might help, but that doesn't mean you won't be attacked.

1. Don't camp near water. That's polar bear territory.

2. Never get between a mother bear and her cubs. Leave immediately, but don't run!

3. Keep food in bear-proof containers.

4. If a bear hisses, pants, or stomps its feet and stares hard at you, back away slowly. Don't look directly into its eyes!

5. Travel in groups of four or more people. Make noise and don't hike at night. That's one of their favorite times to hunt.

6. If a bear stands up, sniffs the air, and moves its head from side to side, it is trying to get your scent. Don't run. Back away slowly.

6

Polar Bear Life

Polar bears do not live in groups. Sometimes they gather to feed on the bodies of dead animals. But except for mothers and cubs, polar bears live alone most of their lives.

Most female bears give birth about every three years. The males and females stay together for a week during the mating season. Afterward they go their separate ways. The females begin

A female polar bear is called a <u>sow</u>.

to eat a lot. They gain over four hundred pounds while they are pregnant!

In the late summer or early fall, they dig dens in the snow. They make sure there is a hole at the top of the den for fresh air. Snow and the warmth of the bears' bodies keep the dens warm during the frigid winter.

Then the female bears curl up for a long hibernation. Eight months later, while they are still hibernating, they give birth to cubs.

Bear Cubs

Newborn bear cubs look like rats without hair. They only weigh about a pound. Their little eyes are tightly shut. It's hard to believe that these helpless creatures become such powerful animals.

At first the new babies sleep close to their mothers and nurse almost all the time.

Most cubs stop nursing at eighteen months.

Growing Up

After the first month, the cubs open their eyes and look around. Their fur and teeth have begun to grow. At two months, they can toddle around in the den.

Mother bears touch and groom their cubs a lot.

When spring comes, mother and cubs leave the den. The mother is hungry. She has not eaten in eight months.

At first the cubs walk slowly. They take time to rest and nurse. When the snow gets too deep, their mother carries them on her back.

The mother bear watches out for male bears. Hungry males will attack and eat weak and helpless cubs.

When the cubs are a few months old, they begin to eat real food. Survival is tough for baby animals. One out of two cubs dies because of lack of food. By eight months, healthy cubs weigh almost a hundred pounds.

Mother bears teach their cubs hunting skills. The cubs watch as their mothers wait for seals to come up to the ice holes. When

Young cubs
catch seals
every five
days or so.

Polar bears
live for about
twenty-five
years.

they are a year old, they begin to try it for themselves.

Early on, they are not the greatest hunters. But by the age of two, they've learned a lot.

Young bears leave their mothers when they are thirty months old. Now they are almost as big as she is. Sometimes the mother even has to chase them away. Their lives as cubs are over. They are big, they have teeth, and they can hunt.

Just Playing

Bear cubs are playful. When a bear cub wants to play, it runs up to another cub. Then it wags its head from side to side. This means: "Come on . . . let's play!"

The cubs fight and wrestle. They race

around and tackle each other. They roll down hills and toss snow at each other.

Sometimes they climb all over their mothers and slide down their sides. And sometimes they get their noses smacked!

Adult males play as well. They "play-fight." In warmer months, males roam the shore waiting for the ocean to freeze. They sleep and rest a lot. Sometimes they look around and find another male to play with. They go up and gently touch him. Then the two wrestle around and try to knock each other down. These fights are tests of strength. The bears seem to be enjoying themselves.

Bad Fights

There are about three males for every female.

During the mating season, fighting is not fun. In order to mate with a female, a male has to fight other males for her.

Before they fight, the bears flatten their ears. Then they put their heads down. They begin to hiss, growl, and roar. Then they attack. The fight ends when one bear gives up and runs away. Although bears can get badly hurt, they almost never fight to the death.

7

The Arctic Is Melting!

Polar bears are in trouble. Our planet is getting warmer. This warming is caused by the burning of coal and oil as fuel. We use these fuels in our cars, houses, and factories. Burning them creates gases that act like a tent around the earth. This invisible tent traps in heat and causes what scientists call *global warming*.

Because the temperature is getting warmer, the sea ice is slowly melting. Polar bears use sea ice for platforms when they hunt for seals. Scientists say the sea ice is melting about three weeks earlier in the year than it did before. Whenever the ice melts, the bears have to stop feeding and head for shore. Because they are not eating as much, polar bears are getting thinner.

Without the right amount of fat, polar bears cannot stay healthy. They are having fewer and weaker cubs.

The melting ice causes another problem. Polar bears can swim far from shore by using ice floes as floats. Because the ice is melting, the distance between the floes is longer. The bears have to swim farther from one floe to another. Some get so tired that they drown.

In September 2004, scientists spotted

four dead polar bears floating sixty miles off the Alaskan coast. Many other bears are feared drowned as well.

Polar bears have other problems besides global warming. They suffer from too much

This 800-mile Alaskan oil pipeline is one of the longest in the world.

hunting by humans and polluted land and water. The number of polar bears is getting smaller. There are only about 22,000 polar bears left in the world today.

Many people are trying to help save the polar bears. They have asked that polar bears be placed on the *endangered species* list. This is a list the government makes of all the animals in danger of *extinction* (ick-STINK-shun). When animals are put on the list, the government tries to protect them and their surroundings.

Extinction means that the animals could die out forever.

It would be a great thing if we could all join together to help save the polar bears. It is hard to imagine the Arctic without them. The wondrous and magical Land of the Midnight Sun would never, ever be the same.

Doing More Research

There's a lot more you can learn about polar bears and the Arctic. The fun of research is seeing how many different sources you can explore.

Books

Most libraries and bookstores have lots of books about the Arctic.

Here are some things to remember when you're using books for research:

1. You don't have to read the whole book. Check the table of contents and the index to find the topics you're interested in.

2. Write down the name of the book.

When you take notes, make sure you write down the name of the book in your notebook so you can find it again.

3. Never copy exactly from a book.

When you learn something new from a book, put it in your own words.

4. Make sure the book is <u>nonfiction</u>.

Some books tell make-believe stories about polar bears and the Arctic. Make-believe stories are called *fiction*. They're fun to read, but not good for research.

Research books have facts and tell true stories. They are called *nonfiction*. A librarian or teacher can help you make sure the books you use for research are nonfiction.

Here are some good nonfiction books about polar bears and the Arctic:

- *Arctic and Antarctic*, Eyewitness Books series, by Barbara Taylor

- *Arctic Tundra*, One Small Square series, by Donald M. Silver, illustrated by Patricia J. Wynne

- *Building an Igloo* by Ulli Steltzer

- *Polar Bears* by Gail Gibbons

- *Polar Bears*, Nature Watch series, by Dorothy Patent and William Muñoz

- *Polar Bear*, Reader's Digest All-Star Readers series, by Sarah Jane Brian and Robert Hynes

Museums and Zoos

Many museums and zoos have exhibits on polar bears and the Arctic. These places can help you learn more about the Arctic and the people and animals who live there.

When you go to a museum or zoo:

1. Be sure to take your notebook!
Write down anything that catches your interest. Draw pictures, too!

2. Ask questions.
There are almost always people at museums and zoos who can help you find what you're looking for.

3. Check the museum or zoo calendar.
Many museums and zoos have special events and activities just for kids!

Here are some museums and zoos with exhibits about the Arctic:

- Alaska State Museums,
  Juneau and Sitka, Alaska

- American Museum of Natural History,
  New York City, New York

- Bronx Zoo and Central Park Zoo,
  New York City, New York

- San Diego Zoo,
  San Diego, California

- Smithsonian National Museum of
  Natural History,
  Washington, D.C.

Videos and DVDs

There are some great nonfiction videos and DVDs about the Arctic. As with books, make sure the videos and DVDs you watch for research are nonfiction!

Check your library or video store for these and other nonfiction titles about the Arctic:

- *Arctic Kingdom: Life at the Edge* from National Geographic

- *Polar Bears: Arctic Odyssey* from Janson Video

- *Really Wild Animals: Polar Prowl* from National Geographic

- *Tasha the Polar Bear* from National Geographic

The Internet

Many Web sites have lots of facts about polar bears and the Arctic. Some also have games and activities that can help make learning about the Arctic even more fun.

Ask your teacher or your parents to help you find more Web sites like these:

- www.enchantedlearning.com/biomes/ tundra/tundra.shtml

- www.geocities.com/mikepolarbear/ parts.html

- www.kidsplanet.org/factsheets/ polar_bear.html

- www.nationalgeographic.com/kids/ creature_feature/0004/index.html

- www.seaworld.org/animal-info/ info-books/polar-bear/index.htm

The word *Arctic* covers a lot of information. It will make your research on the computer and in the library easier if you look up smaller topics like these:

Arctic animals
Arctic Circle
Arctic climate
Arctic people
Global warming
Hibernation
Polar bear cubs
Polar bear diet
Polar bear habits
Tundra

Index

Photos courtesy of:

If you're looking forward to
Dark Day in the Deep Sea,
you'll also love finding out the facts
behind the fiction in

Magic Tree House® Research Guide

SEA MONSTERS

A nonfiction companion to
Dark Day in the Deep Sea

It's Jack and Annie's very own guide to
the creatures of the deep sea!

Look for it March 2008!

Magic Tree House® Books

Other books by Mary Pope Osborne:

Picture books:
The Brave Little Seamstress
Happy Birthday, America
Kate and the Beanstalk
Mo and His Friends
Moonhorse
New York's Bravest
Pompeii: Lost and Found
Rocking Horse Christmas
Sleeping Bobby by Mary Pope Osborne and
    Will Osborne

First chapter books:
The Magic Tree House® series

For middle-grade readers:
Adaline Falling Star
After the Rain
American Tall Tales
The Deadly Power of Medusa by Mary Pope Osborne
    and Will Osborne
Favorite Greek Myths
Favorite Medieval Tales
Favorite Norse Myths

Jason and the Argonauts by Mary Pope Osborne
and Will Osborne
The Life of Jesus in Masterpieces of Art
Mary Pope Osborne's Tales from *The Odyssey* series
Mermaid Tales from Around the World
My Brother's Keeper
My Secret War
The Mysteries of Spider Kane
One World, Many Religions
Standing in the Light
A Time to Dance by Will Osborne and
Mary Pope Osborne

For young-adult readers:
Haunted Waters

MARY POPE OSBORNE and NATALIE POPE BOYCE are sisters who grew up on army posts all over the world. Today, Mary lives in Connecticut. Natalie makes her home nearby in the Berkshire Hills of Massachusetts. Mary is the author of over fifty books for children. She and Natalie are currently working together on *The Random House Book of Bible Stories* and on more Magic Tree House® Research Guides.

Here's what Natalie and Mary have to say about working on *Polar Bears and the Arctic:* "While we were writing this book, we began to worry a lot about global warming. It is happening all over the world. Animals in the Arctic have already begun to feel its effects. Scientists report that polar bears are not able to find as much food as they need. Many are thin and don't produce as many cubs as they did before. Some bears are so hungry they have started to break into houses in search of food. People around the world are calling for ways to help keep polar bears alive. Research on global warming may save them. You see, research isn't just for fun. For some living things, it can mean life or death."